1100 Marks on Foreign Pottery & Porcelain

1st Printing 1937
2nd Printing 1994

L-W Book Sales
P.O. Box 69
Gas City, IN 46933

ISBN# 0-8

D1468403

PREFACE

This manual has been prepared for the guidance of dealers and collectors of antique porcelain and pottery.

It contains only the history and marks of those factories of Continental Europe that are apt to appear on the market under ordinary conditions. They are pieces that will be offered for sale at public auctions, offered to dealers for purchase and offered for sale in the general run of antique shops & malls.

Dealers pass up many fine "buys" through a lack of knowledge of the marks generally found on the bottoms of pieces. Buyers many times pay too high a price for a piece due to the same reason.

When using this book keep in mind it was originally printed in 1937.

MEISSEN

The art of making "true", or hard paste porcelain, was first discovered in Continental Europe, by John Frederic Bottcher, a young chemist in the employ of Augustus II., King of Poland, and Elector of Saxony, in 1709.

The factory was established in the old castle of Meissen, and for the first few years the ware was made only in white, with no colors, and was not sold, but used by the King as presents to his friends.

The first ware was sold at the Leipsic fair, in 1718. The process was kept a secret, and the workmen were all sworn to secrecy, but in 1718 a workman was bribed, and carried the secret of the art to Vienna. From there, in 1720, it was carried to Hochst, in Germany, and then quickly spread over Continental Europe.

Bottcher managed the factory until his death in 1719. Haroldt became director in 1720. Then the King, himself, took the direction, and so continued until his death in 1733.

The history of Dresden, Meissen, or Saxon (the three names given to this porcelain) may be divided into three periods: 1. The Kings Period, ending about 1796; 2. The Marcolini Period, ending 1814; 3. The Modern Period.

The crossed swords of the Arms of Saxony was authorized as the official mark of the factory, in 1721 and is still used.

George Ernst Keil, at Meissen, 1724.

Konigl. Hof. Conditorei Warschan.
1720-1730.

Herold period, 1720.

PORCELAIN OF GERMANY, ETC.

1-8	DRESDEN	Marks stamped on Böttcher red ware.
9, 10, 11	Dresden	Initials of Augustus Rex, in blue and in gold, 1709-'26.
12,13	Dresden	Caduceus mark, on early pieces made for sale, 1717-'20.
14,15	Dresden	King's period, from 1770; the mark with 0 about 1778.
16	Dresden	Crossed swords, with star. Marcolini period, from 1796.
17,18	Dresden	Early marks for (17) *Koniglicher* or (18) *Meissener Porzellan Manufacture.*
19,20	Dresden	First forms of the crossed swords, used from 1719.
21	Dresden	Bruhl's time, 1750.
22	Dresden	Crossed swords; modern mark. The earliest form in Haroldt's period, sometimes closely resembled the modern form.
23	Dresden	A modern mark.
24	Dresden	On a service made for the Countess Cosel.
25	Dresden	Used about 1730.
26	Dresden	Dated 1739.
27	Dresden	Early form of mark.
28,29	Dresden	Mark used 1718.
30,31	Dresden	Early marks
32	Dresden	Mark used 1718.
33	Dresden	Date of use unknown; on statuettes, with or without the crossed swords. (Chaffers.)
36	ELBOGEN	
37,38	SCHLAKENWALD, Austria.	
39-44	HEREND, Hungary	39 is impressed in the paste; 40,41 usually printed in blue; 42, painted in black, with *Herend* impressed; 43, painted in red; 44, initials of M. Fischer.
45,46	ALTEN ROTHAC	*Nowolay,* maker.
47,48	PIRKENHAMMER	*Fischer & Reichembach,* and *Charles Fischer.*
49	PRAGUE	*Kriegel & Co.*
50-53	HÖCHST	Mayence. 51 is the mark of Geltz; 52, of Zeschinger
54	Höchst	Mark of Dahl.

1. B/Z

2. Z

3. AB 1638

4. Matthias Rosa im. Anspach

5. B.K.

6. BK/C

7. B P

8. BP B.P ·BP

9. ᵻ

10. ℛ

11. A F

12. 7ℋ

13. göggingen HS

14. S.

15. G (with wheel symbol)

16. jZ (with wheel symbol)

17. (circled star)

18. (anchor)

19. G: Koxdenbuʃch.

20. GK:

21. AA

22. NB./K:·

23. NB/F

24. NB:/4.

23. Stebner 177; d.13 8bris

24. S

25. ME / u&

26. F. 20/7· 68.P.F. Hm

27. D, 11/4 -10 E

28. HJA

29. B/S

30. ⅄P / 83X

31. F.B.C.F. 1779

32. GHEDT W:I:M J750

34. HL/G

28. A/P/MR

35. :HS:

36. HK N

37. HV XX

39. HV XX

38. ·)

39. CR/N

40. O𝔸

41. F. Pahl·· A𝔖:Π96::

42. PH

43. N Pöʃʃimoer Amno 1725

POTTERY OF SWITZERLAND

1,2.   ZURICH

3.   WINTERTHUR   On an ecritoire. *Jacquemart.*

POTTERY OF GERMANY

4   Anspach (Bavaria).

5,6,7,8,9 BAIREUTH   Sometimes the name in full.

10,11,12   FRANKENTHAL   10 and 11 are marks of Paul A. Hannong;
12, of Joseph A. Hannong. It is not possible to distinguish the first mark from Hannong's when at Strasbourg.

13   GOGGINGEN, near Augsburg, established about 1750.

14   Harburg   Initials of Johann Schaper.

15,16,17   HÖCHST   15 has the G for *Geltz;* 16 the Z for *Zeschinger;*
17 is the wheel alone, the arms of Mayence.

18   POPPELSDORF   Wessel's manufactory; impressed. Also found impressed with the name *Mettlach* on pottery of that place.

19,20,21,22,23 NUREMBERG M. Demmin gives a monogram of H C D, and date 1550, as on a stove. *Glüer,* probably an artist, signs a dish with *Nuremberg. Stroebel* signs a bell, with date 1724, and a dish painted, with date 1730. A stove of green tiles, with religious subjects, has the signature of *Hans Kraut,* and date 1578 Hans Kraut was the great potter of Willingen.

24   SCHREITZHEIM

25,26,27   STRALSUND

28 to 43   Unknown marks on German pottery.

1. FURSTENBERG The F is made in various forms.
2. HESSE CASSEL?
3. HESSE DARMSTADT (Jacquemart)
4,5. FULDA
6. GERA? or GOTHA?
7,8. Gotha
9. WALLENDORF (Also used at Berlin)
10. ARNSTADT
11,12,13,14. LIMBACH

15. VOLKSTADT. Marryat says KLOSTER VEILSDORF. *See 24, below*
16. ANSPACH. So says Marryat. *See 26,46,47,48 below*
17. RAUENSTEIN
18,19. GROSBREITENBACH
20. Grosbreitenbach?
21,22,23. RUDOLSTADT. R was used in various forms.
24. Volkstadt. *See 15, above*
25. Gera. Two forms of G.

26. Attributed to Gera and to Anspach: probably the latter. Chaffers gives it with a D under a crown. The mark varies from a rude eagle (46) to this form. *See 16*

27,28. BADEN-BADEN. The blade of an axe or two axes, in gold or impressed.

29-35. LUDWIGSBURG (KRONENBURG). The double C is the eipher of Charles Eugene, who died 1793, but the mark was used till 1806. It must not be confounded with that of Niderviller, in Custine's time, which was sometimes accompanied by a coronet. The mark frequently appears without the crown, as in 31 and 32. The form 30 (L with a crown) is also a mark of the time of Charles Eugene. The letters CC in mark 29 were changed in 1806 to T.R., the T.R. being sometimes in monogram; and in 1818 the letters W.R. were substituted. The stag's horns, singly, 35, or on a shield, as in 34, were also used.

36. HILDESHEIM, HANOVER. Sometimes the letter A only; from about 1760.

37,38,39. NYMPHENBURG AND NEUDECK. The first is the oldest mark. These are impressed, without color, and sometimes difficult to recognize. Found on pieces with marks of other factories, which bought and decorated them.

40-45. FRANKENTHAL. 41, P.A. Hannong's mark; 42, Joseph A. Hannong; 43, initials of Carl Theodore, Elector; 44, supposed, of Ringler; 45, supposed of Bartolo.

46,47,48. Anspach, in Bavaria.
49. BAIREUTH

50. REGENSBURG (RATISBON).
51. WURTZBURG, Bavaria.

52-57 BERLIN The sceptre is the general mark, made in several forms, 52, 53, 54 are the earliest marks of *Wegeley*, 1750-'61; 56, globe and cross and K.P.M., for *Königlicher Porzillan Manufacture*, adopted about 1830; 57, modern mark, alone, and with K.P.M. The Wegeley marks resemble Wallendorff and others.

58. CHARLOTTENBERG
59. PROSKAU
60. VIENNA

61. SCHLAKENWALD, Austria
62,63,64. Unknown marks on German hard-paste porcelain.

9

MARKS, ETC., OF GERMANY, SWEDEN, DENMARK, SPAIN, PORTUGAL

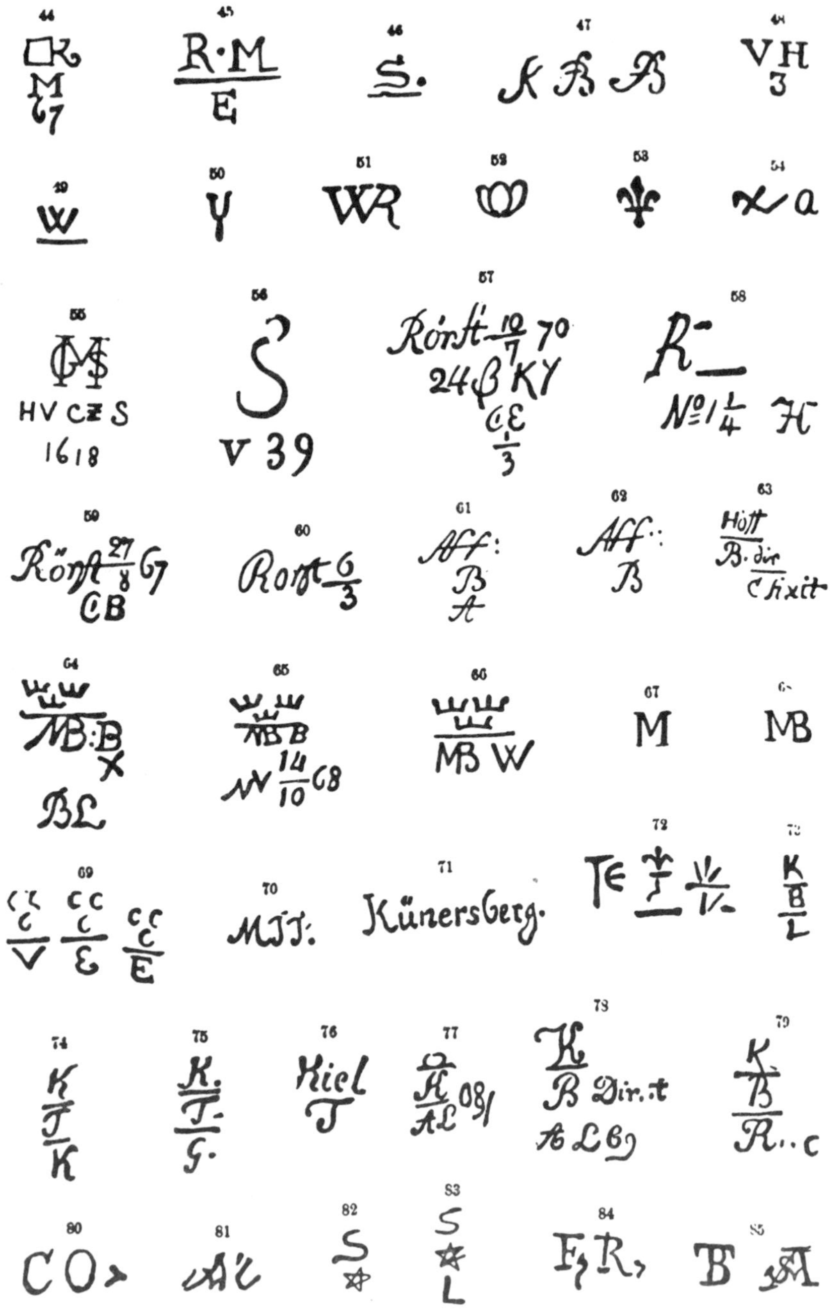

44-56. Unknown marks on German pottery.

POTTERY OF SWEDEN, ETC.

57-62. RORSTRAND. 61 and 62 are probably signatures of *Arfinger,* according to Mrs. Palisser. Chaffers gives a mark, *Storkhulm* 22, 8. 1751 *D H B,* as of the factory after Rorstrand was united to Stockholm. The marks include the date, price, and signatures of artists. *Stockholm* is found, and also *Rorstrand,* impressed.

63. Rorstrand, or Marieberg, or Kiel?

64-69. MARIEBERG.

70. Swedish?

71. KÜNERSBERG.

72. Künersberg?

GUSTAFSBERG, 1820 to 1860. The mark is the name with an anchor.

HELSINBURG. Given by Mr. Chaffers as on stone-wares, made from 1770.

73-79. KIEL.

POTTERY OF SPAIN AND PORTUGAL

80,81. ALCORA.

82,83. Attributed to SEVILLE.

84,85. LISBON.

VIENNA

The Vienna factory was the first to make hard paste porcelain, after Dresden, Claude Innocent Du Pasquir receiving a twenty-five year patent in 1718, from the Emperor, Charles VI. He hired a Meissen workman by the name of Stenzel. Stenzel's work was poor. He refused to reveal the secret of the process for making hard Paste porcelain. He quit and the factory was abandoned.

Du Pasquir, in some way, learned the secret, and again opened the factory, but not meeting with the success that he expected, sold the factory, and the secret, to the government, then under the rule of Queen Marie Theresa.

From then on, the factory prospered. From 1780 to 1820, it's artists equaled, and even surpassed, those of Dresden and Sevres. Such noted artists as Leithner, Wech, Raffey, Foerstler, Lamprecht, Joseph Nigg, Perger, Shallez, Varsanni, and Herr, were employed. The factory ceased operations in 1864.

The mark was always the shield of the Arms of Austria, in different forms. From 1784 to 1864, the last three numerals of the year of manufacture were impressed in the paste, as 796 for the year 1796, etc.

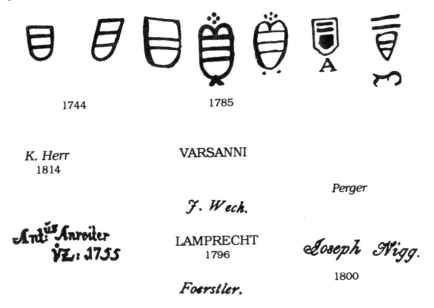

1744   1785

K. Herr
1814

VARSANNI

Perger

J. Wech.

Andⁱᵘˢ Anreiter
ṼⅬ: 1755

LAMPRECHT
1796

Joseph Nigg.
1800

Foerstler.

12

Sèvres

Sèvres was the continuation of a factory that was originally established at Vincennes, in 1738. It was moved to Sèvres in 1756.

Old Sèvres is much sought after by collectors, and commands high prices. The ware is so marked that it is easy to name the exact age of any piece. The factory is still in operation.

DATE MARKS OF SEVRES

MARKS USED AT SÈVRES TO INDICATE DATES OF MANUFACTURE

A (Vincennes)	1753	N	1766
B "	1754	O	1767
C "	1755	P	1768
D "	1756	Q	1769
E "	1757	R	1770
F "	1758	S	1771
G "	1759	T	1772
H "	1760	U	1773
I "	1761	V	1774
J (see footnote)	1762	X	1775
K	1763	Y	1776
L	1764	Z	1777
M	1765		

AA	1778	JJ	1787
BB	1779	KK	1788
CC	1780	LL	1789
DD	1781	MM	1790
EE	1782	NN	1791
FF	1783	OO	1792
GG	1784	PP	1793
HH	1785	QQ	1794
II	1786	RR	1795

This mode of marking the date fell into disuse, and, from this period until 1800, it is found only on rare examples. In 1801, the custom of dating was resumed, and the letters replaced by the following signs:

T.9	An IX (1801)	9	1809
X	" X. (1802)	10	1810
II	" XI. (1803)	oz. (onze)	1811
-II-	" XII. (1804)	d. z. (douze)	1812
	" XIII. (1805)	t. z. (treize)	1813
	" XIV. (1806)	q. z. (quatorze)	1814
7	1807	q. n. (quinze)	1815
8	1808	s. z. (seize)	1816
		d. s. (dix-sept)	1817

From 1818 the year is expressed by the two last figures only. Thus: 18=1818, 19=1819, etc., and is so continued to the present time.

PORCELAIN OF SÈVRES

1. **Vincennes.** The interlaced double L, the initial of the king's name, was adopted by the Vincennes factory shortly after its foundation, and used till 1753. The mark, unaccompanied by other letters, is rarely, if ever, found on porcelain made at Sèvres. After the removal of the factory to Sèvres, this mark, accompanied with date letters, as hereafter explained, continued the typical mark of the factory down to the Revolution.

2. Vincennes. The mark was usually in this form, with a dot in the monogram. Marks 1 and 2 should be found only on pieces made prior to 1753.

3. Vincennes and Sèvres. In 1753, at Vincennes, the system of dating by letters of the alphabet was adopted, A being 1753, B 1754, etc. See *Table of Marks used to indicate Dates*. The factory was removed to Sèvres in 1756. A,B,C,D, therefore, date wares of Vincennes. D also dates work at Sèvres. The date letter is placed either within or outside of the monogram, and is sometimes a capital and sometimes a small letter.

4. The crown was adopted over the monogram as the mark of hard-paste porcelain after its introduction. Forms of this mark are 5,6, and 10, showing accompanying signatures of artists. Thus, mark 10 includes the factory mark, the device of the artist *Vieillard*, and the date DD, 1781. This mark on a service in the T.-P. collection has also the mark of another artist, *Bavdoin*, on each piece.

7. The letter Z having been reached in 1777, double letters were used thereafter, AA being 1778, etc. A difference of opinion exists as to whether the letter J was used for 1762, but the best authorities now agree that it was used.

8,9. In the Republican period the royal initial was abandoned, and the mark R.F., for *République Franquise*, was adopted (1792-1800), always accompanied by the word *Sèvres*. The R.F. was in monogram, as in mark 8, or in one of the forms in mark 9. Dates were not used from 1792 to 1801.

11. About 1800 the word Sèvres was used alone, without the R.F. It was usually in a form similar to mark 11, but varied as made by different hands. This mark was in use from 1800 till the end of 1802.

12. In the Consular period, 1803, the mark 12, for *Manufacture Nationale*, was used, stencilled in red.

13. In the Imperial period, beginning May 8th, 1804, mark 13, for *Manufacture Imperiale*, was adopted, and used till 1809, stencilled in red.

14. The imperial eagle was adopted as the mark in this form in 1810, printed in red, and continued in use till the abdication, in 1814. Date marks were used from 1801, for which see *Marks used to indicate Dates*.

15. Mark of the period of Louis XVIII., used from May, 1814, to September, 1824, the date indicated by the last two figures of the year. This mark was printed in blue.

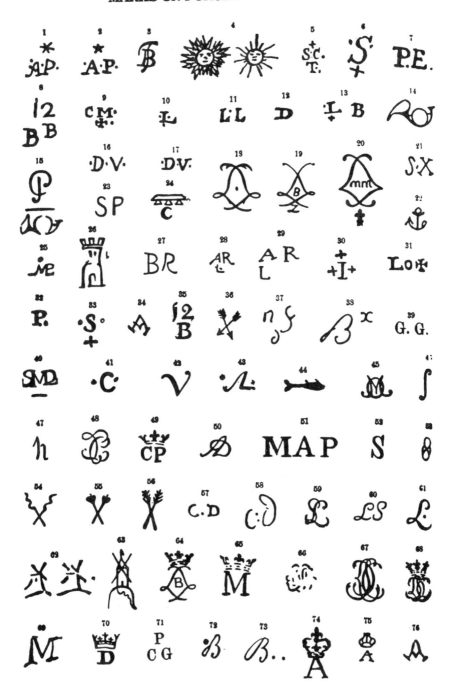

PORCELAIN OF FRANCE

1,2.   Unknown marks on early French porcelains, given by Jacquemart as possibly Louis Poterat, of Rouen, 1673-1711.

3.   Unknown, on similar porcelain.

4.   St. Cloud. Two forms, *Pierre Chicanneau*, 1702-'15.

5.   St. Cloud. Trou, 1706.

6,7,8.   Uncertain. On porcelains resembling St. Cloud.

9.   Paris. *Marie Moreau*, widow of Chicanneau's son.

10-13.   Lille. 10 is the earliest mark. In 13 L is on a saucer, and B on the cup.

14,15.   Chantilly. 15 is Pigorry's mark since 1803.

16,17   Mennecy-Villeroy.In gold, color, and later impressed.

18,19,20.   Vincennes and Sèvres. See marks on Sèvres.

21,22,23.   Sceaux. 21 usually scratched. 22 later, painted in blue. 23 scratched

24. Orleans.	26. La Tour d'Aigues.	28,29. Arras
25. Etiolles.	27. Bourg-la-Reine.	

30-39.   Unknown marks on early French porcelains, resembling St. Cloud, given by Jacquemart. 33, 35 are doubtless the same as 6,8 above.

40-46.   Unknown marks on hard-paste porcelains. 44 attributed by Riocreux to Fontainebleau. 45 resembles the mark of a Sèvres painter.

47.   Paris. Pierre A. Hannong's mark, 1773.

48,49.   Paris, same factory. Charles Philippe.

50.   Paris. Gros Caillou. Established by Lamarre, 1773.

51.   Paris. Morelle à Paris. Established 1773.

52,53.   Paris. Souroux, potter. Established 1773. His successor was Ollivier.

54.   Paris. De la Courtille factory.

55.   Paris. De la Courtille. This mark, torches or headless arrows, is made in various forms, and sometimes resembles the Dresden crossed swords.

56   Paris. *Dubois*. This mark – two branches, alluding to the maker's name – often resembles the previous one. Also assigned to De la Courtille factory.

57,58.   Limoges. Factory of Massie. The earliest mark was G.R. et Cie.

59,60.   La Seinie. Established 1774.

61.   Paris. J.J. Lassia, 1774.

62-70.   Clignancourt. The windmill is the earliest mark, rare, used only in 1775. 64 is stencilled on a specimen. 65, initial of *Mousieur*, the king's brother; 66, 67, 68, initials of Prince Louis Stanislas Xavier; 69, initial of Moitte director, used with the name *Clignancourt;* 70, initial of Deruelle, director.

71.   Paris. *Manufacture du petit Carousel.* Mark used with the name of the factory variously abbreviated.

72,73.   Boissette.

74,75,76.   Paris. Lebeuf. *Porcelaine de la Reine.* Initial of Marie Antoinette.

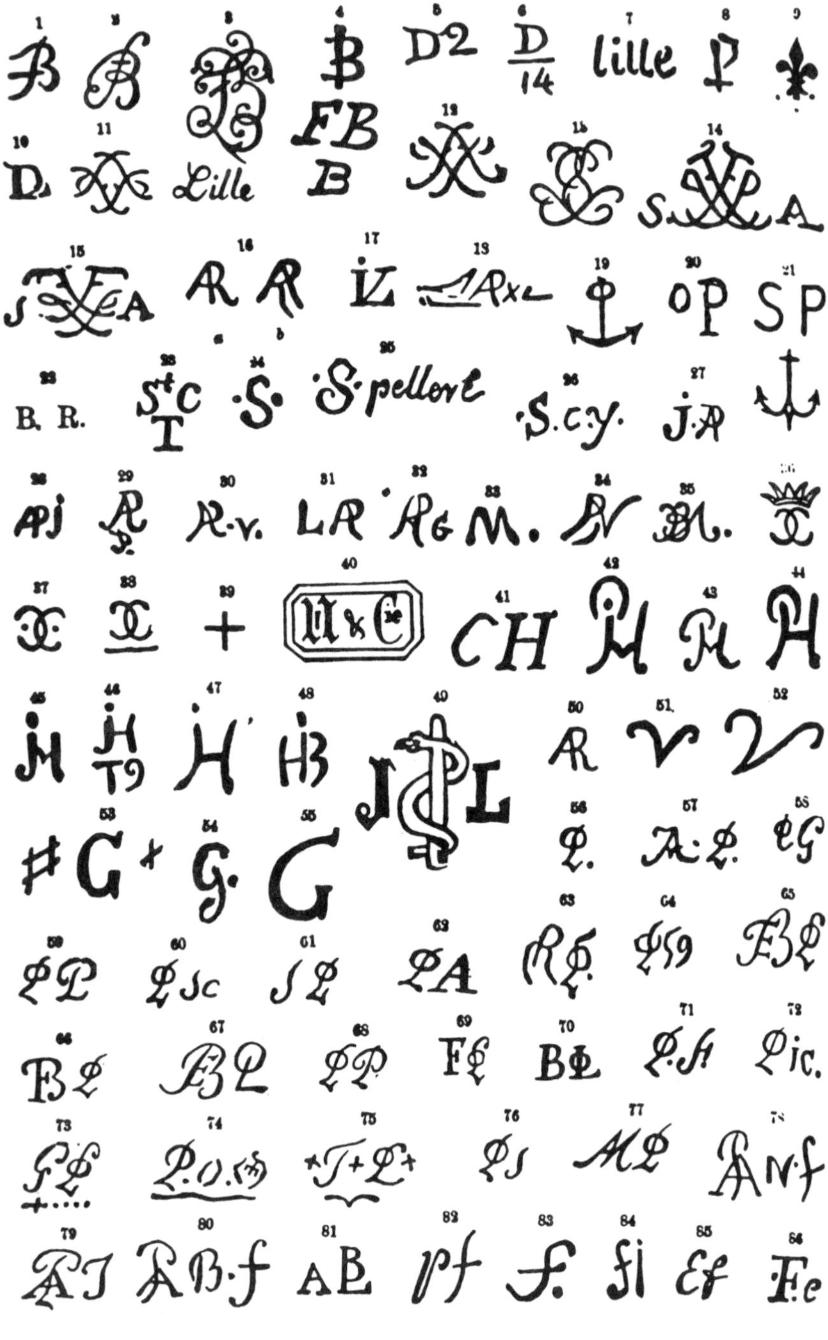

FRANCE

1,2,3. LILLE. Francois Boussemart.

4. Lille. Febvrier and Boussemart?

5,6. Lille. Barthelemi Dorez, 1709-'15. His grandson signed *N.A. Dorez*, in 1748.

7,8,9. Lille; 7, about 1788; (?) 8, Petit?

10. VALENCIENNES. *Louis Dorez.*

11,12,13,14,15. ST. AMAND LES EAUX. *P.J. Fauquez.*

16. PARIS. *Claude Reverend's* mark.

17,18. Paris. On ware resembling Reverend's.

19. SCEAUX. Mark of Glot, who also marked with the word SCEAUX. Prior to 1772 the mark had been S X.

20. Sceaux? or Bourg la Reine? Doubtful.

21. Sceaux. Glot's period.

22. BOURG LA REINE.

23. ST. CLOUD. *Trou's* mark.

24,25,26. SINCENY. 25 is signature of *Pellevé*, director.

27,28,29,30,31,32. APREY. The factory monogram Ap, with initials of Jarry and other artists.

33. MATHAUT.

34,35. NIDERVILLER. Beyerlé period. The mark is B N in monogram.

36,37,38,39. Niderviller. Custine period. These marks must not be confounded with Kronenburg, or Ludwigsburg.

40. SARREGUEMINES. *Utzchueider & Co.*

41. STRASBOURG.*Charles Hannong.*

42,43,44. Strasbourg. *Paul Antoine Hannong.*

45,46,47. Strasbourg. *Joseph Adam Hannong.*

48. Strasbourg or Hagenau. Possibly *Balthasur Hannong.*

49. PREMIERES, in Burgundy. *J. Lavalle.* Other marks are J L P in a script monogram.

50. MEILLONAS. *Madame de Marron.*

51,52. VARAGES.

53,54,55. TAVERNE. *Gaxe*, director.

56-86. MOUSTIERS. The marks including a monogram of O L are attributed to Joseph Olery. Some are his, but Jacquemart doubts many. 86 is supposed signature of Fouque, successor to Clarissy. Names, perhaps, of Spanish artists – *Soliva, Miguel Vilax, Fo Gianzel, Cros* – occur. A potter, *Ferrat*, about 1760 signs his name. *Pierre Fournier* signs work dated 1775; *Antoiue Guichard*, in 1763: *Thiou*, in the last century. *Moustiers* appears as a mark written and also applied through pricked points.

87 *A.*   88 *F*d   89 *F*d   90 *G*   91 *M.C.*   92 *M·C·A1756·J·A*   93 *P.F.*

94 *F·P*   95 *·oy·*   96 ⚜   97 ⚜   98 ⚜   99 *R*   100 *R*   101 *R*

102 *·R·X·*   103 *V?*   104 *V*   105 *B.*   106 *F.*   107 *R*   108 *M*   109 *M*

110 *R*   111 ♛   112 *J. Boulard a Nevers* 1622   113 *DLF* 1636   114 *JB*

115 *HB* 1689   116 *H·B* 1689   117 *S.*   118 *P.C*   120 *E.Borne* 1689   119 *de conrad A neuers*

121 *·F.R.1734*   122 *N*   124 *A·+ Limoges ⚬ Le 18 me may J74J*

123 ✶   ✶ ✶   125 ♜   *de Conrade a ntuers*

126 *avisseau a tour 1855*   127 *A·C A*   ☀   128 *AN*   129 *A· P·*   130 *A / E*

132 *CD CABRI 1762*   131 *R*   133 *CB*   134 *·C· :S:*   135 *δ*   136 *F*   137 *F.C- 1661*

143 *GDG 1780 1/2*   138 *FFc FSc*   139 *F E.*   140 *f.f.*   141 *GAA*   145 *H*

142 "Fait par GDE, A no 1761."   146 *HE*   144 *H G I*

87-95. Moustiers. 87 and 88 are marks of *Feraud*, potter. 95 is probably Olery. The other marks are uncertain.

96-98. MARSEILLES. The fleur-de-lis is attributed to *Sary* after 1777.

99-102. Marseilles. *J.G. Robert.*

103,104. Marseilles. *Veuve Perrin.*

105. Marseilles.*A. Bonnefoy.*

106. Marseilles. *J. Fauchier.*

107. MARANS. *J.P. Roussency.*

108,109. Marans.

110. RÈNAC. (Jacquemart.)

111. ORLEANS.

112-123. NEVERS. 112 is the earliest known signature; 113, Denis Lefebvre; 114, Jacques Bourdu; 115, 116, Henri Borne on statuettes; 117, Jacques Seigne; 119, Dominique Conrade, third of the name, 1650-'72; 120, Etienne Born; 121, Francois Rodriguez; 122, Nicholas Viodé; (?) 123, from the Conrade arms.

124. LIMOGES. Massie.

125. LA TOUR D'AIGUES.

126. *Arisseau,* modern potter at Tours (died 1861).

127-146. Unknown marks on French pottery.

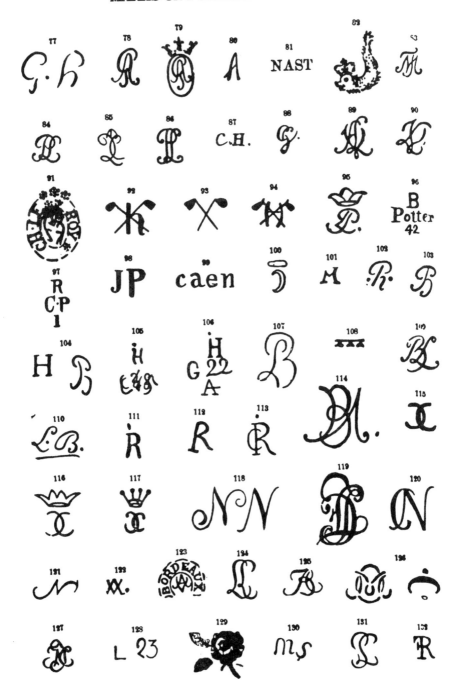

FRANCE

77. Paris. *Porcelaine de la Reine*. Initials of Guy & Housel, successors to Lebeuf. These occur with *Rue Thirou à Paris*. LEVÈILLE, 12 *Rue Thiroux*, is the latest mark.

78,79,80. Paris. *Porcelaine d'Angoulème*. Early marks of *Guerhard & Dihl*. Later marks are their names in full, and MANUFACTURE DE MONS. LE DUC D'ANGOULÈME À PARIS, without name.

81. Paris. *Nast*, manufacturer. Stencilled.

82. LILLE. The early pieces have *à Lille*.

83,84,85,86. Paris. Factory established by Lamarre, 1784.

87,88. Paris. II.F. Chanou. Established 1784. The marks are pencilled in red.

89,90. VALENCIENNES. Initials of Fauquez, Lamoninary, and V. Early mark, *Valencieu*.

91. CHOISY LE ROY. Impressed.

92,93,94. Vincennes.

95. Vincennes. Attributed to Hannong's, or another factory under the patronage of Louis Philippe.

96,97. Paris. Charles Potter. *Porcelaine du Prince de Galles*.

98. Paris. Belleville, Jacob Pettit. The J has sometimes a dot above it.

99. CAEN. Desmare et Cie. Established 1798.

100. Paris. *Manufacture de S.M. l Impèratrice*. Also marked with full name of factory, and *P.L. Dagoty*, proprietor.

101-106. STRASBOURGE. 101, C. Hannong; 102,103, Paul A Hannong; 104, the same, with II in the paste; 105, J.A. Hannong, with numbers; 106, J.A. Hannong.

107. BRANCAS LAURAGAIS.

108,109. ORLEANS.

110. Given by Jacquemart as the mark of Jacques Louis Broilliet on experimental porcelain, at *Gros Caillon* (Paris), 1765.

111,112,113. MARSEILLES. Robert. 113 is doubtful.

114-121. Niderviller. 114, Beyerle's period; 115,116, 117, 120, Custine's period. These marks must not be confused with Ludwigsburg. 119 is Lanfray's cipher. NIDERVILLE in an open outlined letter is impressed on statuettes of Franklin and other biscuit pieces.

122,123. BORDEAUX. Marks of Verneuille

124. Unknown French. Resembles Limbach, in Germany.

125-131. Unknown marks on French porcelain.

132. Attributed by Baron Davillier to Marscilles.

BOW

The first soft-paste porcelain established in England, was established at Stratford-le-Bow, commonly known as "Bow", about 1730. Little is known of the products of this factory, until 1744, when Edward Heylin and Thomas Frye received a patent to make porcelain.

Bow made some of the finest of the English porcelains, services, vases, candelabra, shell and rock work, statuettes, and groupes.

A characteristic of this ware, is the thickness of the glaze, which is somewhat milky, and fills up the finer lines in reliefs. The colors are delicate, and color combinations in birds, insects and flowers, lend a remarkable beauty to this ware.

There were no regular factory marks for Bow ware. Arrow-marks, bows, daggers, and many other marks and designs are found, that will be of no use to the collector in authenticating a specimen. Many Bow pieces were reproduced at the Chelsea and Derby works, as were also the Bow marks. The best way to absolutely authenticate your piece, is by comparison with an authenticated piece of Bow.

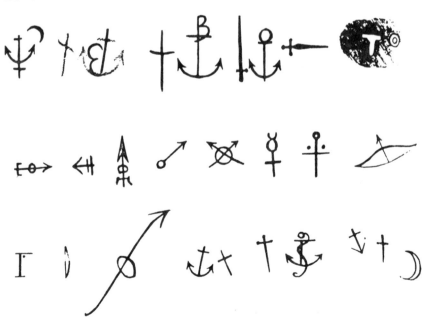

CHELSEA

The factory at Chelsea was founded about 1745, by the Duke of Cumberland and Sir Evard Fawkener. The manager was Nicolas Sprimont, who afterward became the proprietor, when he purchased the factory in 1755.

In 1769, Duesbury, of Derby, bought the works, and ran them in connection with the Derby plant, until 1784, in which year he combined the two plants, in Derby.

The best period of Chelsea, was from 1750, to 1765. The products were of great beauty, and excellence. Candelabra, with foliage and groups of figures; animals under trees, and other figures. The paintings were of the finest. From 1760 to 1763 the turquoise, deep blue, crimson, apple-green and claret color grounds of Sevres was copied with great success. This ware is highly prized, and much sought after, by collectors.

Forms of the anchor mark in colors or gold.
The anchor was used by many other factories.

DERBY 1750-1937

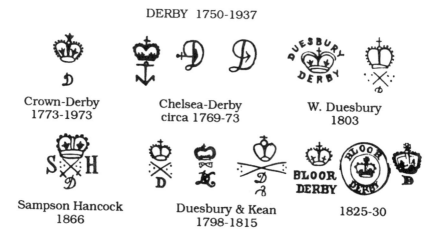

Crown-Derby
1773-1973

Chelsea-Derby
circa 1769-73

W. Duesbury
1803

Sampson Hancock
1866

Duesbury & Kean
1798-1815

1825-30

Present mark interlaced script D's under crown. Words "Trade Mark" underneath. Words "Royal Crown Derby" over crown.

Bristol

Pottery was made at Bristol as far back as 1700, at a factory owned by Richard Frank. Joseph Ring founded the BRISTOL POTTERY, in 1784, and this name appears on his ware. He also used a simple cross mark in blue, or lead color.

From 1768, to 1782, Richard Champion made hard-paste porcelain.

Characteristic of this ware, is numerous bubbles and pinholes, also spiral ridges formed by the fingers of the potters in turning the wares on the potters wheel.

These same characteristics appear on the ware made at Plymouth.

Champion copied many of the decorations of the Dresden and Sèvres factories, and used the crossed swords of Meissen as a mark on the Dresden copies.

While this ware is not as desirable, from an artistic standpoint, as some of the other continental porcelains, it's scarcity, and rarity make it a valuable addition to any collection.

**Bristol Porcelain
First Period (1750)**

(1765-1782)

This mark is in slight relief

Between 1772 and 1774

Tebo's mark

BRISTOLL 1750

Bristol

This mark is in slight relief

Lowestoft

Soft-paste porcelain was made at Lowestoft as early as 1756, and up to 1762. This ware was in imitation of Delft, in blue and white.

Between 1762 and 1804, this factory made a fine porcelain closely resembling the Chinese. In fact, many collectors contend that no porcelain was ever made at Lowestoft, it being made in China, and the decorating done in this factory. But that contention has been proven false by the characteristicly English decorations on pieces held in some of the English Museums, and marked, under the glaze "Allen, Lowestoft", the signature of Robert Allen, an English painter, of that period.

The marks given herewith, are ascribed to Lowestoft. They are, presumably, the marks potters, and decorators, as no standard mark, as far as is known, was ever used by this factory.

$$J \quad \underline{V} \quad IV \quad VI \quad 3 \quad \cdot \quad 5 \quad 16 \quad \phi \quad 4^{\ell} \quad 110 \quad cnx$$

Swansea

A pottery was established by George Haynes at Swansea, in Wales, in 1750, for the manufacture of ordinary wares. In 1800, he made a ware called "opaque china", which was, in reality, a vitreous earthen-ware.

In 1802, the works were sold to Lewis W. Dilwyn. From this date, and until 1817, such noted decorators as W.W. Young, and William Billingsley were employed, and the ware produced during this period is classed as some of the finest ever produced in England. The works were bought by a Mr. Rose in 1820, and transferred to Coalport.

Swansea SWANSEA

ENGLAND

98.   COALPORT.

99-104. COLEBROOK-DALE. The first three are the older marks. 102, adopted 1851. 103, is the modern mark, being a monogram of S.C., for Salopian, Colebrook-Dale, and including C, for Caughley or Coalport; S, for Swansea; and N, for Nantgarrow, the combined factories.

105.   SHELTON. The *New Hall* factory. Modern marks of this factory are HACKWOOD, or HACKWOOD & Co., from 1842 to 1856; then C & H, *late Huckwood*, for Cockson & Harding; and since 1862 HARDING.

106-110. PINXTON.

111-132. WORCESTER.The early mark is the letter W, in various forms, as in 112. This stands for Worcester or Wall.

The crescent, also in different forms, as in 113, in blue, gold, or impressed, was used prior to 1793. It must not be mistaken for the crescent of Caughley, which it closely resembles, so that specimens can sometimes be identified only by the paste or the decorations.

The marks numbered 111 are workmen's marks. These do not identify specimens with certainty, as of Worcester, for similar marks are found on other porcelains.

The square marks 114, 115, 116, are early marks, imitating Oriental.

Marks 117, 118, 119 are found on prints, and are the signatures of Robert Hancock, engraver. The anchor in 118 and 119 may be of Richard Holdship. See text.

The marks 120-126 are early marks, fanciful imitations of Chinese. Other marks occur, resembling these in character.

127,128,129,130.   are imitations of the crossed-sword mark of the Dresden factory.

131.   is an imitation of the mark of Sèvres.

132.   is an imitation of the mark of Chantilly.

133-146. WORCESTER (continued from previous page). Flight purchased the works (1783), and used his name, impressed (mark 133), or painted (134), sometimes with the crescent mark in blue. 133 and 134 were used till 1792. After the king's visit, in 1788, mark 135 was sometimes used.

136. Scratched mark of Barr after 1793.

137. Flight & Barr, 1793-1807.

138,140. Flight, Barr & Barr, 1807-'13. The F.B.B. impressed.

139. Impressed mark, used 1813-'40.

141. Printed mark, used 1813-'40.

142. Chamberlain, 1788 to about 1804.

143. Chamberlain, 1847-'50. Impressed or printed.
   A printed mark, *Chamberlain's Regent China, Worcester, etc.*, under a crown, was used from 1811 to about 1820.
   A written mark, *Chamberlains, Worcester, & 63 Piccadilly, London, was used about 1814.*
   A printed mark, CHAMBERLAINS, WORCESTER, & 155 NEW BOND ST. LONDON, under a crown, was used from 1820 to 1840. After the union of the two factories in 1840, the printed mark was CHAMBERLAINS & Co., 155 NEW BOND ST., & No. 1 COVENTRY STREET, LONDON, under a crown.
   In 1847 the mark was simply *Chamberlain & Co., Worcester.*
   From 1847 to 1850 mark 143 was used.

144. Was used 1850-'51

145. Mark adopted by Kerr & Binns, 1851, and since used.

146. Kerr & Binns, on special work.

147. PLYMOUTH. In blue, red, or gold.

148-164. BRISTOL. The general mark is a cross (149), in slate-color, blue, or in the paste, with or without numbers and other marks. Numbers from 1 to 24 are thought to be of decorators. B, with a number (marks 151-154), was frequently used. 155 shows Bristol and Plymouth combined; 157, John Britain., foreman in the factory. 159 shows an embossed T over the cross in blue. The Dresden mark was frequently used, as in 160, 161, 162, 163, in combination with numbers, etc. 164 is probably a workman's mark.

165-169. STOKE. *Minton.* 165 is the earliest mark. 166, 167 are also early marks, 168 was used about 1850, and 169 later.

170-174. Stoke. Marks of Josiah Spode, father and son. 170 is an old mark, neatly pencilled in various colors.

175

176

177

178

179

180 COPELAND

181 COPELAND

182 Copeland late Spode

183

184 ROCKINGHAM

185

186 SWANSEA

187 CAMBRIAN

188 NANT-GARW G.W.

189 DAVENPORT

190

191 P

192 ROGERS

193 Mason's Patent Iron Stone China.

194 Opaque China B and C

195

196

197 M & N

198

199

200 Absolon yarm

201 C G

202

203 LEEDS POTTERY

204 TURNER

205 SCOTT PB

206 HERCULANEUM

207

208 HERCULANEUM

209 WEDGWOOD

210 WEDGWOOD & BENTLEY ETRURIA

211 Wedgwood & Bentley

212 Wedgwood

213 Wedgwood & Bentley

214

175-183. Stoke. Marks of the several successors of Spode since 1833.

175. Copeland & Garret, 1833-'47.

176. Used by Copeland & Garret.

177. Copeland & Garret.

178,179. Copeland & Garret, 1833-'47.

180. Copeland, 1847-'51.

181. Copeland after 1851.

182. Copeland used, 1847-'67.

183. W.T. Copeland & Sons after 1867.

184. ROCKINGHAM. Adopted about 1823. The mark of *Brameld* from 1807 was his name impressed, sometimes with a cross and four dots. Teapots have impressed marks: MORTLOCK, CADOGANS, MORTLOCK'S CADOGAN, ROCKINGHAM. Coffee-pots had sometimes the pattern name NORFOLK impressed.

185. SWANSEA. The name SWANSEA, stencilled or impressed, was used about 1815; also SWANSEA, DILLWYN & Co., and DILLWYN'S ETRUSCAN WARE. Marks 185, 186 are impressed, date unknown. 187 is on an old pottery vase, *Cambrian Pottery* also appears.

188. NANTGARROW, 1813-'20, painted, impressed, or stencilled. *Mortlock*, in gilt, occurs on ware decorated in London, and also on Swansea ware.

189. LONGPORT. *Davenport's* mark. The earliest mark was LONGPORT, or DAVENPORT LONGPORT. The marks are impressed or printed, and forms vary. After 1805, on iron-stone wares the anchor was in a portico.

190. LIVERPOOL. *Richard Chaffers.*

191. Liverpool. *Pennington, in gold or colors.*

192. Longport. *Rogers.* Pottery and iron-stone.

193. LANE DELPH. *C.J. Mason.* Various other marks, including the name. The oldest marks include the name, MILES MASON; a mark is MASON'S CAMBRIAN ARGIL; and the late mark, FENTON STONE WORKS, C.J.M. & Co.

194. TUNSTALL and BURSLEM. *Bridgwood & Clark, 1857.*

195. LONGTON. *Hilditch & Son.*

196. Tunstall. *Bowers?*

197. Longton. *Mayer & Newbold.*

198,199. On Elers-ware teapots.

200. YARMOUTH. *Absolon.*

201,202,203. LEEDS. 201 is *Charles Green.*

204. LANE-END. *Turner.*

205. EDINBURGH (Portobello) pottery.

206,207,208. Liverpool. 206, 208 are Herculaneum pottery. Marks of this pottery are found impressed, painted, and printed on bottoms and sides of pieces.
207 is of *Case & Mart*, proprietors from 1833.

209-214. BURSLEM and ETRURIA. Marks of *Wedgwood* and his factory. The most common mark is the word WEDGWOOD, impressed. This is continued in use.

ENGLAND

53-57.   Bow? These marks occur in blue on figures.

58.   Bow? Supposed monogram of Fry in blue.

59.   Bow? Impressed.

60.   DERBY. On service made for the Persian ambassador.

61.   Derby. On a plate.

62.   Derby. Used in 1842. Imitation of Sèvres.

63-76.   Derby. On various pieces. 71-75 are marks of Cocker, on figures, etc., made by him at Derby till 1840, and after that in London; 76 is an imitation of a Sèvres mark.

77-82.   WORCESTER. Workmen's marks on Worcester porcelain.

83.   CAUGHLEY. Forms of the crescent mark, and C in blue.

84.   Caughley. Forms of S, for Salopian, in blue or impressed.

85.   Caughley.

86,87.   Caughley.

88-96.   Caughley. Numerals 1,2,3, etc., in fanciful style on printed wares.

97.   Caughley. Mark of Rose?

Worcester

Dr. John Wall, a physician, founded the Worcester porcelain factory in 1751, his associates being the Rev. Thomas Vernon, Richard Holdship, and others.

In 1772, this company was sold out, and was purchased by the Rev. Mr. Vernon for a new company, which consisted of Dr. John Wall, William Davis Senior, William Davis Junior, Rev. Thomas Vernon, Robert Hancock, the engraver, and Richard Cook.

In 1783 the works were sold to Joseph, and John Flight. In 1793, Martin Barr was taken into the firm, and the firm name was "Flight & Barr". In 1807 another Mr. Barr came into the firm, and the name was changed to "Barr, Flight & Barr".

In 1783, Robert and Humphrey Chamberlain, who were employed, left the firm and established a rival factory.

In 1840, the Chamberlain, and Worcester factories were combined, under the name "Chamberlain & Co.". In 1852, Kerr & Binns bought the company; and in 1863, a company known as "The Worcester Porcelain Company" was organized. This company is still in operation.

Collectors of fine porcelain consider "Old Worcester" as one of the finest of all the continental wares. Those of "Dr. Wall", "Flight & Barr", and "Barr, Flight & Barr" periods, are very rare, and are much to be prized.

Wedgwood

The wedgwoods were potters at Burslem. Aaron Wedgwood was the first potter of this famous family, and was born some time about the middle of the seventeenth century. The ware made by this family through the seventeenth and eighteenth centuries was of the common varieties of those times, and no interest is connected with their products, until we reach Josiah Wedgwood, who was born in Burslem, in 1730.

The history of this great family of potters is too long to be given in this book. Pieces marked "WEDGWOOD & BENTLY. ETRURIA" (1768-1780) marked "WEDGWOOD ETRURIA". "WEDGWOOD" (printed in blue or red) (1805-1815) "WEDGWOOD" (alone) (1768-80) "WEDGWOOD" (under picture of vase) (1878) "JOSIAH WEDGWOOD, SONS, & BYERLEY" (1790-1823) "JOSIAH WEDGWOOD & SONS (1823). In this year the name was changed to "JOSIAH WEDGWOOD & SON".

The factory is still in operation, and the ware is marked "WEDGWOOD" and since 1891, with the word "ENGLAND" added to conform with the law passed in this country, at that date as to the marking of wares imported into the United States from other countries.

Minton

In 1790, Thomas Minton established a pottery at Stoke. He made pottery until 1798, when a ware called "Semi-transparent China" was introduced. This ware produced until 1811, and then abandoned, and resumed in 1821. In 1817, Herbert Minton, his son, entered the firm as a partner. Thomas Minton died in 1836, and his son became sole owner.

Minton has always been a fine ware, and collectors should buy it, whenever possible. The factory is still in existence.

Meigh

Job Meigh bought the pottery of Christofer C. Whitehead, in 1780. The mark on the ware is MEIGH. The factory ceased in 1860. Ware marked "MEIGH, OLD HALL" is always a good buy.

E. Mayer, & E. Mayer & Son

Elijah Mayer established a factory in Hanley, in 1770. The factory ceased in 1830. Much ware from this firm was shipped to America. The mark E. MAYER, dates from 1770, to 1813. That marked E. MAYER & SON, from 1813, to 1830. JOSEPH MAYER & CO. early 19th century. T.J. & J. MAYER, MAYER BROS., and MAYER & ELLIOT, from 1830, onward.

Adams

William Adams opened a factory at Tunstall, about 1780. He made copies of Wedgwood, that in some cases were as good as the originals. The ware was marked ADAMS & CO. (1770-1790), ADAMS, (1787-1810) W. ADAMS & CO. (1786-1790) on jasper ware. ADAMS, EST'BD. 1657. TUNSTALL, ENGLAND. This last mark used since 1891. The factory is still in existence.

Mason

Miles Mason made pottery at Lane Delph the latter part of the 18th century. Other Mason marks are, "C.J. MASON & CO. LANE DELPH." (1800-1805) "FENTON STONE WORKS". (1805) "M. MASON". "MASON'S CAMBRIAN-ARGIL". "MASON'S IRON STONE CHINA". "MASON'S PATENT IRON STONE CHINA". "MILES MASON", AND "MASON'S CAMBRIAN ARGIL", are late 18th century marks. Mason's works and rights were sold to Ashworth Bros. in 1859.

Spode

Josiah Spode established a factory at Stoke-upon-Trent, about 1770. William Copeland was made a partner in 1779. Up to the year 1800, only pottery was made. In this year, Spode's son, who had succeeded him in the business, started to manufacture the now famous Spode porcelain. The elder Spode died in 1797, and his son, in 1827. The Spode factory is still in business, owned and managed by the descendants of the original William Copeland.

Spode has always been noted as a fine ware, and the old Spode is eagerly snapped up by collectors.

Ridgway

Job Ridgway & Sons were potters at Shelton before 1814, when the sons John and William Ridgway succeeded Job. They made both pottery, and porcelain, the mark being J.W.R. The more modern mark is J.R., for John Ridgway. Brown, Westhead Moore, & Co., are the modern proprietors.

J. & R. Clews

This firm were potters at Cobridge from 1814 to 1836.

They catered to the American market, with ware decorated with American scenes and pictures of noted Americans. They made cream ware in relief patterns and colors, but blue seems to have been the favorite color for this market. Pieces of Clews in good condition, are well worth having.

Wood

Aaron Wood opened a factory in Burslem in 1750. Enoch Wood, his son, began business in 1784. In 1790, James Caldwell entered the firm, and the firm became "WOOD & CALDWELL". Caldwell retired in 1818, and Wood took his three sons into the firm. The firm continued under the name "E. WOOD & SONS" until it was closed in 1846.

PORCELAIN OF ITALY, SPAIN, AND PORTUGAL

1. FLORENCE. On Mediccan porcelain. The arms of the Medici, and initials of Franciscus Medici Magnus Etruriae Dux Secundus.

2. Florence. On Medicean porcelain. Dome of the Cathedral.

3. Tablet held by a lion, in the decoration of a bowl. See text.

4,5,6,7. DOCCIA, near Florence.

8,9,10,11. LE NOVE. 10 and 11 are signatures of *Gio. B. Antonibou.*

12,13. VENICE. *Vezzi;* impressed, or in red.

14,15,16. Venice. *Cozzi;* in red, blue, or gold. This mark must be distinguished from that of Chelsea in England.

17. Venice.

18-26. NAPLES; CAPO-DI-MONTE factory. 18 is supposed to be the earliest marks in blue. The fleur-de-lis was also used at the Buen Retiro factory in Madrid, as given below. 21,22,23,24 are marks of Ferdinand IV in and after 1759. The crowned N is often reversed in the mark. The marks are sometimes in color, sometimes impressed.

        GIUSTINIANI of Naples made hard-paste porcelain using the same marks as on pottery; see p. 451.

27-31. MADRID. Marks of the Buen Retiro factory. This factory was an outgrowth of Capo-di-Monte in Naples, and used the fleur-de-lis mark also. 27 and 28 are the cipher of Charles III. 29 is M for Madrid.

32. VISTA ALLEGRE, near Oporto, Portugal.

33,34,35. TURIN, Italy; Vineuf factory of Dr. Gionetti, impressed or scratched. The cross is also sometimes accompanied by scratched lines, forming VN in monogram.

POTTERY OF BELGIUM

1-3. TOURNAY. Marks, probably of Peterynck.

4. TERVUEREN.

5. MALINES. Attributed by Jacquemart.

6. BRUGES. *Henri Pulinx.*

7. LUXEMBOURG. Mark of the brothers *Boch* before the French Revolution.

8. Luxembourg. Subsequent mark impressed.

9,10. Luxembourg.

11-19. Unknown marks on Flemish pottery.

POTTERY OF HOLLAND

20. AMSTERDAM, 1780-'83, *Hartog v. Laun.*

21-40. DELFT.

21. *Samuel Piet Roerder.*

22,23,24. *Suter van der Even,* 1580.

28. Factory with sign of *De Metaale Pot,* 1639.

29,30. *De Paauw* (The Peacock), 1651.

31. *Jacobus de Milde,* 1764.

32. *Martinus Gouda.*

33. *Q. Kleynoven,* 1680

34. *Cornelius Keyser, Jacobus Pynaker,* and *Adrian Pynaker,* 1680.

37. *Jan Jansz Kuylick,* 1680.

38. *Johannes Mesch,* 1680.

39. *T Fortuyn* (The Fortune), 1691.

40. Widow of Pieter van der Briel.

41 IB 42 D 43 *130 44 AK 45 AK 46 I D A 47 DVD

48 Roos 49 D 50 L.S / 7 51 52 WD 53 ITD / 12

54 DEX 55 Z :DEX. 18 / 2 56 I H D 57 Hooren 58 M

59 VK 60 E. B. S. 61 GVS 62 GVS 63 RH

64 65 b9 66 JB 68 HVMD 5

69 THART 70 thart 71 P 67 B 2 72 Duijn

73 puijn 74 v duijn 75 De Blompot 76 PD

77 D. S. K. 78 PP Kan 79 LPK 80 P 81 W. V. B.

HOLLAND

41-81. Marks deposited in the Hotel de Ville, Delft, in 1764, by potters designating their shop names. These are not always given in facsimile.

41-45. DE WITTE STER (The White Star). *A Kielle.*

46. IN DER VERGULDE BOOT (The Gilded Boat). *Johannes der Appel.*

47-49. DE ROOS (The Rose). *Dirk van der Does.*

50. DE KLAAUW (The Claw). *Lambertus Sanderus.*

51,52. DE DRIE KLOKKEN (The Three Bells). *W. van der Does.*

53-56. DE GRIEKSE A (A Greek A). *J.T. Dextra.* 1765 the works passed to *Jacobus Halder Adriuensz* (M. 56).

57. DE DRIE PORCELEYNE ASTONNEN (The Three Porcelain Barrels). *Hendrick van Hoorn.*

58,59. DE ROMEYN (The Roman). *Petrus van Morum.* The same year the manufactory passed into the hands of *Jan van der Kloot Jausz* (M.59).

60. T'JONGUE MORIAANS HOFFT (The Young Moor's Head). Widow of *Peter Jan van der Hagen.*

61-63. IN T'OUDE MORIAANS HOFFT (The Old Moor's Head). *Gectruy Verstelle.*

64,65. DE PORCELEIN BYL (The Porcelain Hatchet). *Justus Brouwer.* Occurs frequently.

66,67. DE DRIE PORCELEYNE FLESCHJES (The Three Porcelain Bottles). *Hugo Brouwer.*

68-70. T'HART (The Stag). *Hendrik van Middeldyk.*

71. DE TWEE SCHEERJES (The Two Ships). *Anth. Pennis.*

72-74. DE PORCELEYNE SCHOOTEL (The Porcelain Dish). *Johannes van Duyn.*

75. DE VERGULDE BLOMPOT (The Gilded Flower-pot). *P Verburg.* The mark is not facsimile.

76. DE PORCELYN FLEN (The Porcelain Bottle). *Pieter van Doorne.*

77. DE DUBBELDE SCHENKKAN (The Double Pitcher). *Thomas Spaandouck.*

78-80. DE LAMPETKAN (The Ewer). Widow of *Gerardus Browner.*

81. DE TWE WILDEMANS (The Two Savages). Widow of *Willem van Beek.*

GERMANY, HOLLAND, SWITZERLAND, BELBIUM, RUSSIA, ETC.

65-76. Unknown marks on German hard-paste porcelain.

77,78. Uncertain; possibly Frankenthal, *Hannong fecit.*

79. Weesp, Holland.

80. Weesp? Arnstadt? Saxe Gotha? Uncertain.

81. Loosdrecht. Manufactur oude Loosdrecht.

82,83. Amstel (Amsterdam).

84. Amsterdam. The lion frequently alone.

85. The Hague.

86,87,88. Brussels. 87 is mark of L. Cretté.

89-92. Luxembourg. 93 is the modern mark.

93. Zurich, Switzerland

94. Nyon, Switzerland

95-98. Tournay. 95 is Peterynck's mark from 1751; the tower is also assigned to Vincennes, and pieces thus marked are called "Porcelaine de la tour."

99,100,101. Marieberg, Sweden.

102,103. Copenhagen. Three waving lines for the Sound and the Belts.

POTTERY AND PORCELAIN OF RUSSIA, ETC.

104-112. St. Petersburg. Royal factory; 104, time of Empress Elizabeth, 1741; 105, 106, Empress Catharine (Ekaterma); 1762; 107, Emperor Paul, 1796; 108, Emperor Alexander, 1801; 109, Emperor Nicholas, 1825; 110,111, Emperor Alexander II., 1855; 112, shows system of dates by dots adopted 1871 – one dot for 1871, two for 1872, etc.

113,114. St. Petersburg. Brothers Korniloff.

115-119. Moscow. Gardners.

120-123. Moscow. Popoff. Factory established 1830.

124. Kiev, Russia, or near there at Mejigorie. Pottery.

125. Baranowka, Poland. Pottery.

126. Chmeloff, Poland. Pottery.

127. Kiev, Russia. Pottery.

128. Korzec, Poland. Pottery.

Marks of Periods.

德建	Ken-tok, 1370.
中文	Bun-tin, 1372.
授天	Ten-du, 1375.
和弘	Ko-wa, 1380.
中元	Gen-tin, 1380.
四德明	Mei-tok, 1393.
永廳	O-yei, 1394.
長正	Show-tiyo, 1428.
享永	Yei-kiyo, 1429.
吉嘉	Ka-kitsu, 1441.
安文	Bun-an, 1444
德宝	Ho-tok, 1449.
德亨	Kiyo-tok, 1452.
正康	Ko-show, 1455.
祿長	Chiyo-rok, 1457.
正寬	Kwan-show, 1460
正文	Bun-show, 1466.
仁廳	O-nin, 1467.
明文	Bun-mei, 1469.
亨長	Chiyo-kiyo, 1487.
德延	En-tok, 1489.
廳明	Mei-o, 1492.
龜文	Bun-ki, 1501.

Marks of Periods.

正永	Yei-show, 1504.
永大	Dai-jei, 1521.
祿亨	Kiyo-rok, 1528.
永大	Di-yei, 1532.
冶弘	Ko-dsi, 1555.
祿永	Yei-rok, 1558.
元	Gen-ki, 1570.
正天	Ten-show, 1573.
祿文	Bun-rok, 1592.
長慶	Kei-chiyo, 1596.
和元	Gen-wa, 1615.
永寬	Kwan-jei, 1624.
保正	Show-ho, 1644.
安慶	Kei-an, 1648.
廳承	Show-o, 1652.
曆明	Mei-reki, 1655.
冶萬	Man-dsi, 1658
文寬	Kwan-bun, 1661.
寶延	Yen-po, 1673.
和天	Ten-wa, 1681.
享貞	Tei-kiyo, 1684.
祿元	Gen-rok, 1688.
永寶	Ho-yei, 1704.

Marks of Periods.

德正	Show-tok, 1711.
保享	Kiyo-ho, 1717.
文元	Gen-bun, 1736.
保寬	Kwan-po, 1741.
享延	Yen-kiyo, 1744.
延寬	Kwan-jen, 1748.
曆寶	Ho-reki, 1751.
和明	Mei-wa, 1764.
永安	An-Jei, 1772.
明天	Ten-mei, 1781.
政寬	Kwan-sei, 1789.
和享	Kiyo-wa, 1801.
化文	Bun-kwa, 1804.
政文	Bun-sei, 1818.
保天	Ten-po, 1834.
化弘	Ko-kua, 1844.
永嘉	Ka-yei, 1848.
久文	Bun-se, 1854.
冶元	Man-yen, 1860.
廳慶	Bun-kin, 1861.
冶明	Gen-di, 1861.
政安	Kei-o, 1865.
延萬	Mei-di, 1868.

MARKS ON JAPANESE POTTERY AND PORCELAIN

Shiba (Tokei) Pottery

 Hikomakoro, maker at Sie-un-tei, in Shiba.

 Unknown.

Awari Porcelain

 Awari.

 Saeng-ets; beautiful moon; name of celebrated painter.

Ai-we, name.

 Spring Mountain.

 Painter's name (Yama-moto Sho-tan)

Symbols, Inscriptions, Names, etc.

 Long life.

 Long life.

Symbols, Inscriptions, Names, etc.

 Happiness

 Wealth.

 So-o.

 Kami, maker.

Rakou-masa, maker.

 Huzi-nori, name.

 Imitation of Chinese marks "Precious property of Jo shin."

 Shin-fo-se-seki, name.

 Seven honorable societies.

 Hall of increase of peace, harmony.

 Wealth, honors, and long youth.

 Wealth, honors, and long life.

Hezen Porcelain

肥前 } Hezen, or Fisen.

肥州 } He-shu.

田肥 ヵ前 三有 } Hezen: Haritikami, maker.

信肥 南修 造山 } Hezen: Shinpo, maker.

佺尺 目淏 並山 } Hezen: Reksen, maker.

西肥 南里有山 製 } West Hezen: Nan-di, maker.

百太造 肥前有田 } He-shu (Hezen): Tentai, maker. Haridan, factory.

The following are hezen factory villages:

山内侑大 Great mountain between rivers.

山内侑三 Three mountains between rivers.

山泉和 Mountain of springs.

平髙攵 Beautiful upper plain.

平野本 Beautiful chief plain.

平野中 Middle plain.

平長 Long plain.

Hezen Porcelain

郎大 Great vase.

郎中 Medium vase.

川白 White stream.

町赤 Street of painters in red.

屋岩 The cave.

剗南 South bank.

尾囧 Outside tail.

田乇黑 Black field.

瀨廣 Firo-se

瀨ノ一 Iteche-na-se.

左井 Imali.

Kaga Pottery and Porcelain.

九谷 } Kutani: the nine valleys.

九釒 } Kutani.

▮ } Kutani.

▮ } Made at Kutani.

九谷造 } Made at Kutani.

 } Kagayo Kutani.

九谷加湯 } The same.

加湏 } The same.

MARKS ON JAPANESE POTTERY AND PORCELAIN

Kaga Pottery and Porcelain

 } Kagayo Kutani.

 } Great Japan, made at Kutani.

 } Kutani Bok-zan.

 Kutani: Touzan.

 Porcelain Mountain (Touzan).

 Rising-sun Mountain.

 Ponzan.

 Dio, maker.

 Great Japan; Garden Mountain; strong pottery.

 To-o.

 } Made at Kutani, long house.

 Kutani.

Kaga Pottery and Porcelain

 Long life.

 Happiness.

 Riches.

Kioto Pottery.

 } Kioto.

 } Kioto, Japan; Kinkousan, maker.

 Kinkousan, maker.

Satsuma Pottery.

 Itsigaya, a place

Tai-zan, maker.

 Tai-zan.

 } Tai-zan.

 } Tai-zan.

 Den-ko, name.

Enamel Marks

 } Enamel mark. Forgery (?) of Chinese date 1645.

 } Di-Nipon: Great Japan

Han-suki, maker. (Enamel)

 } Nipon: Japan. Next signs illegible.

Eurok, maker. (Enamel)

Awata Potteries.

 } Great Japan

Dioto, maker.

 Tokio, name of factory; and

Maker's names.

 Ae-rako, a name.

 Ki-yo, a name.

 Yu-ah-su-zan, a name.

 } Awata.

Banko Potteries.

 } Banko.

 Banko.

Banko Potteries

 Nipon, Japan.

Ari-nori, name.

 Banko.

 Shing-en, a name.

 Banko.

 Banko.

 Banko: eminent of flowers.

 Banko, an old mark.

 Guso, name.

 Maker's mark.

 } Bishu.

 } Hiradoson.

Shi-ac, maker.

 } Hiradoson, and

maker's name.

MARKS ON JAPANESE POTTERY AND PORCELAIN

Symbols, Inscriptions, Names etc.

Symbols, Inscriptions, Names etc.

Wealth, honors, and long life.

Made at beautiful garden.

The same: maker's name (Gos-ki) added.

 On ware probably Hezen.

Chinese mark of 1426 on Hezen ware.

Chinese mark of 1465 on Hezen ware.

Great Japan; Hirak, maker.

Pavilion of Spring

Tsi-tze, maker.

 Same factory name.

Sanfo, maker. These are on Nagasaki wares.

 Sito in Japan, with maker's name; Nagasaki.

 Hata, factory.

 Middle mountain.

 Itsi-yama.

 These and many other square marks are found on blue painted wares.

MARKS, ETC., ON PORCELAIN OF CHINA

Marks of Periods.

明大 Ta Ming Dynasty, 1368-1647.

武洪 Hung-woo, 1368.

文建 Keen-wan, 1399.

樂永 Yung-lo, 1403.

熙洪 Hung-he, 1425.

德宣 Seuen-te, 1426.

統正 Ching-thung, 1436.

泰景 King-tae, 1450.

順天 Theen-shun, 1457.

化成 Ching-hwa, 1465.

治弘 Hung-che, 1488.

德正 Ching-tih, 1506.

Marks of Periods.

靖嘉 Kea-tsing, 1522.

慶隆 Lung-king, 1567.

歷萬 Wan-leih, 1573.

昌泰 Tac-chang, 1620.

啓天 Theen-khe, 1621.

禎崇 Tsung-ching, 1628.

光弘 Tsung-kwang, 1644.

武紹 Shaou-woo, 1647.

武隆 Lung-woo, 1647.

曆永 Yung-leih, 1647.

清大 Ta Thsing Dynasty. 1616-1861

Marks of Periods.

命天 Theen-ming, 1618.

聰天 Theen-tsing, 1627.

德崇 Tsung-te, 1636.

始順 Shun-che, 1641.

熙康 Kang-he, 1662.

正雍 Yung-ching, 1721

隆乾 Kien-long, 1736.

慶嘉 Kea-king, 1796.

光道 Taou-kwang, 1821.

豐咸 Han-fung, 1851.

冶同 Thung-she, 1861.

MARKS IN THE SEAL CHARACTER

 Shun-chee, 1644.

 Kang-he, 1662.

 Yung-ching, 1723.

 Kien-long, 1733.

 Kea-king, 1796.

 Taou-kwang, 1822.

 Han-fung, 1851.

 Thung-che, 1861

 Ching-hwa, 1465. Forgery on modern work

 Shun-che, 1644. Another form of four marks.

 Kien-long, 1736. Another form

 Taou-kwang, 1822. Another form

 Han-gund, 1851. Another form

 Thung-che, 1861. Another form

 Thung-che Name only.

54

CHINESE MARKS AND SYMBOLS

Marks, Symbols, etc.

Three forms of the two-fish mark, found on old blue ware; one of the earliest known, from 969-1106.

The sesamum flower. Various flower marks are found, in ancient and modern periods.

Hoa: a small flower inside a cup. Marks the Yung-lo period, 1403-1424.

Butterfly.

Show: long life; a wish for longevity, common in one or another of these and other forms on porcelain: sometimes repeated a

Marks, Symbols, etc.

hundred or more times. Such pieces are called "hundred show."

Circular show mark.

Oval show mark.

Thin form of show.

Fuh-che; happiness.

55

Marks, Symbols, etc.

祥萬
製明　} Wan ming cheang (name) che (made).

御雍
製正　} Yung ching yu che: made for Yung ching.

奇連
后成　} Leen ching khe how (not translated).

珍若
藏深　} Jo shin chin tsang; precious property; Jo shin (name).

斗垂
甄涤　} Same mark.

珍莊
秋珠　} Same mark.

鼎奇石寶
之珍　} Ting Khe che she chin paou — Ting of very precious and costly stone.

鼎奇玉宝
之珍　} Ting Khe che she chin paou — Same meaning.

玉思
雅有美
製　} Yuh Chung ya yuh che mei — For the true-hearted elegant gem made.

福壽比
如南
東海山　} Long life as the south mountain. Happiness like the east sea.

Marks, Symbols, etc.

 Badge of authority; on pieces for mandarines.

 Tablet of honor, including the Swatika. (See text).

 Another form of the same.

 Another form.

 A mandarin mark of honor.

 The sounding-stone. (See text).

 Another sounding instrument.

 Sacred axe. (See text).

 Shell (see test) or helmet (?).

 Shell (?).

 Shell (?).

 Standard table.

 Leaves, frequent marks.

 Treasures of writing, stone for ink, brushes for writing, a roll of paper, etc. Found as a mark; and common, as are many of the previous designs, in the surface decorations of porcelain.

Marks, Symbols, etc.

Marks, Symbols, etc.

Beautiful vase for the wealthy and noble. Otherwise translated: wealth, honors, and intellect.

Probably a name.

Valuable vase for divining.

Bamboo leaves, used as a mark at King-te-chin. 1573-1619. We have also found the leaves used as an exterior decoration of porcelain dishes which we believe to be Persian.

These three combinations, or arrangements of lines, known as the eight diagrams of Fuh-hi, frequently occur on Chinese porcelain. They have reference to certain mystic ideas, utterly unintelligible to us, relating to the genders, the principles of creation, the origin of all things, etc., etc. Chinese philosophers profess to understand their meaning and suggestions, and the Chinese regard them as talismanic.

Square marks, common on old specimens, in these and many other forms.

Paou: precious.

American Pottery

The history of American pottery, and porcelain, is rather vague, until about the middle of the 18th century. It is known that pottery was made in Virginia, as early as 1650, but no specimens of this ware are in existence.

There were also, a few small potteries in South Carolina, but due to the fact that none of the ware of that day was marked with the makers name, it is impossible to give any exact data on this ware.

In 1735, a John Remmey conducted a pottery in the city of New York. He died in 1762, and was succeeded by his son, John Remmey II. A Mr. Clarkson Crolius also made pottery there in the latter part of the 18th century. The pottery was closed in 1848.

The Germantown works were started in 1753 by Joseph Palmer, who came to this country from Devonshire, England in 1746. With him was associated his wife's brother, Richard Cranch. The firm made both pottery, and glass, the glass consisting of bottles of all sizes, and in large quantities.

In 1770 a pottery was started in Philadelphia, by a group headed by Gousse Bonnin, a former workman at the Bow factory in England. With him was associated George Anthony Morris. It may be said that here starts the history of American porcelain. The works closed in 1774.

It is not possible that the collector will ever be able to find a piece of pre-revolutionary ware that can be authenticated as such, so therefore, further history of this period will be of little use, and we will pass on the period beginning in the early part of the 19th century.

American Pottery

After the revolution many of the old, and an increasing number of new potteries started operations. In fact, by the year 1879, there were more than seven hundred plants in America. As practically none of the ware was marked, until about 1828, a list and dates of the factories up to this date (1829) will be of little use to the collector. A very complete history of American pottery and porcelain can be obtained in Kovels' New Dictionary of Marks on Pottery & Porcelain.

The following are the known marks, used from the year 1829 up to 1890.

ROOKWOOD (Cincinnati)

Jacob Scholl
1830

The addition of a flame
each year makes
the 1895 mark.

Tucker & Hulme
China Manufacturers
Philadelphia
1828

Tucker & Hulme
1828

Manufactured
by Jos Hemphill
Philad—

Jos. Hemphill
1832

ℛ

1887

D & J
Henderson
Jersey
City

D. & J. Henderson
1829

AMERICAN
POTTERY CO
JERSEY CITY

American Pottery Co.
1840-1845

ℛ

1886

**ROOKWOOD
1882**

**NORTON & FENTON
East Bennington, Vt.**

Norton & Fenton
1845-1847

C. W. Fenton
1847-1848

American Marks

Edwin Bennett
1856

Lyman & Fenton
1849-1858

·· J.M. & Co.

John Moses & Co.
1863

Salamander Works
1848

A.P.M. Cᵉ

American Porcelain
Manufacturing Co.
1854-1857

Smith & Son
1876

United States Pottery Co.
1853

CHELSEA KERAMIC
ART WORKS
ROBERTSON & SONS

Chelsea Keramic
Art Works
Chelsea, Mass.
1866-1889

Southern Porcelain Co.
1856-1864

Griffen, Smith & Hill
Phoenixville, PA
1879

BELLEEK

Otter & Brewer
1876

O.-B.
CHINA

Otter & Brewer
1866

New England Pottery Co.
1878-1895

Faience Manufacturing Co.
New York
1886

A Few Don'ts

If you are attracted to a beautiful piece that is unmarked, don't pass it up on that account. Many fine pieces went into the kiln unmarked, through carelessness of a workman. Buy the piece if reasonably priced, hold it, and some day you will find a similar piece that is marked, and then you will be able to authenticate your prize.

There is a word that always "types" the amature. That word is "reproduction". Don't use it. If you think the piece is not an original, call it a copy.

Many famous factories, at some period, turned out some very inferior work. Don't always buy the factory mark. Collect your specimens from a standpoint of beauty, as well as from a historical viewpoint.

Many potteries, in the old days before a trademark could be copyrighted, would copy the mark of some famous potter, and issue it on very inferior ware. If you are collecting, say Meissen, get an authenticated piece, and use it for comparison. At least seventeen other potteries used the Meissen crossed swords, in one form or another. Constant handling, and study of the modeling paste and decoration of the genuine piece, will soon give you what is known as the "feel", and you will be able to detect the copy without trouble.

Forged Marks

Meissen

The crossed swords mark was taken from the coat of arms of Saxony, and were first used as a mark, by the Meissen Factory. Copies of Meissen pieces were made, and the mark copied, by the following factories.

Germany
Berlin – 1751-61.
Anspach – 1760.
Wallendorf – 1762.
Rauenstein – 1760.
Dornheim – 17th century.

Belgium
Tournay – After 1755.

France
Montreuil – 1815.
Paris – Jacob Petit

Holland
Weesp – 1764.
Backhuyzen – 1741.

History

Meissen 3
Vienna 12
Bow 24
Chelsea 25
Bristol 26
Loestoft – Swansea 27
Worcester 36
Wedgwood – Minton 37
Mayer, Meigh, Adams, Mason 38
Spode, Ridgway, Clews, Wood 39
American Pottery 58
American Pottery – Rookwood 59
A Few Don'ts – Forged Marks 61

Marks

Page 3-4-5-12

Germany .... Dresden
.... Hochst
.... Mayence

Austria .... Schlakenwald
.... Vienna

Hungary .... Herend

Bohemia .... Elbogen
.... Alten Rothau
.... Prague

Page 6-7

Switzerland .... Zurich
.... Winterthur

Germany .... Anspach
.... Baireuth
.... Frankenthal
.... Goggingen
.... Harburg
.... Hochst
.... Poppelsdorf
.... Nuremburg
.... Schreitzheim
.... Stralsund

Page 8-9

Germany .... Furstenberg
.... Hesse Cassel
.... Hesse Darmstadt
.... Fulda
Gera, or Gotha
Wallendorf
Arnstadt
Limbach
Volkstadt
Kloster Veilsdorf
Anspach
Rauenstein
Grosbreitenbach
Rudolstadt
Volkstadt
Gera
Baden-Baden
Ludwigsburg
Hildesheim
Frankenthal
Anspach
Baireuth
Berlin
Charlottenberg
Proskau
Vienna
Schlakenwald

Marks

Page 10-11

Sweden .... Rostrand
.... Marieberg
.... Kunersberg
.... Gustafsberg
.... Kiel

Spain .... Alcora
.... Seville

Portugal .... Lisbon

Page 13-23

France .... 11-12-13- Sèvre
.... St. Cloud
.... Paris
.... Lille
.... Chantilly
.... Mennecy-Villroy
.... Vincennes-Sèvres
.... Sceaux
.... Orleans
.... Etiolles
.... Arras
.... Limoges
.... La Seinie
.... Clignancourt
.... Boissette
.... Valenciennes
.... St. Armand Les Eaux
.... Bourg La Reine
.... Sinceny
.... Aprey
.... Mathaut
.... Niderviller
.... Sarreguemines
.... Strasbourg
.... Premieres
.... Meillonus
.... Varages
.... Taverne
.... Moustiers
.... Marseilles
.... Marans
.... Renac

.... La Tour d'Aigues
.... Choisy Le Roy
.... Brancas Lauragais
.... Bordeaux
.... Paris

Page 24
.... Bow

Page 25
.... Chelsea

Page 26
.... Bristol

Page 27
.... Loestoft
.... Swansea

Page 36
.... Worcester
.... Coalport
.... Coalbrook-Dale
.... New Hall
.... Pinxton

Page 30
.... Worcester
.... Plymouth
.... Bristol
.... Minton
.... Spode

Page 32
.... Spode
.... Copeland
.... Copeland and Garrett
.... Rockingham
.... Swansea

Marks

Page 32 continued

.... Swansea
.... Nantgarrow
.... Longport
.... Liverpool
.... Mason
.... Bridgwood & Clark
.... Hilditch & Son
.... Bowers
.... Mayer & Newbold
.... Absolon
.... Leeds
.... Turner
.... Scott
.... Herculaneum
.... Wedgwood

Page 34

.... Bow
.... Derby
.... Worcester
.... Caughley

Page 42

.... Tournay
.... Tervueren
.... Malines
.... Bruges
.... Luxembourg
.... Amsterdam
.... Delft

Page 40

.... Florence
.... Doccia
.... Le Nove
.... Venice
.... Naples-Capo-Di-Monte
.... Giustiniani
.... Madrid
.... Vista Allegre
.... Turin

Page 45

.... Delft
.... Holland factories

Page 47

.... Switzerland
.... Belgium
.... Germany
.... Russia
.... Holland Etc.

Page 48-53

.... Japanese

Page 54-57

.... Chinese

Page 58-60

.... American